D0579188

UNDERSTANDING SEXUAL ORIENTATION AND GENDER IDENTITY

Other Books in the LIVING PROUD! Series

LIVING PROUD! GROWING UP LGBTQ

UNDERSTANDING SEXUAL ORIENTATION AND GENDER IDENTITY

Robert Rodi and Laura Ross

Foreword by Kevin Jennings
Founder, GLSEN (the Gay, Lesbian & Straight
Education Network)

MASON CREST

Mason Crest
450 Parkway Drive, Suite D
Broomall, PA 19008
www.masoncrest.com

Printed in the United States of America

First printing
9 8 7 6 5 4 3 2 1

Series ISBN: 978-1-4222-3501-0
Hardcover ISBN: 978-1-4222-3511-9
ebook ISBN: 978-1-4222-8384-4

Cataloging-in-Publication Data is available on file at the Library of Congress.

Developed and Produced by Print Matters Productions, Inc. (www.printmattersinc.com)
Cover and Interior Design by Kris Tobiassen, Matchbook Digital

Picture credits: 10, The Yorck Project/Wikimedia Commons; 12, pkline/iStock; 15, Herkie/Wikimedia Commons; 16, Sean Buck/Fotolia; 19, Zakir Hossain Chowdhury/ZUMA Press/Newscom; 21, Wikimedia Commons; 24, czarny_bez/iStock; 27, Stephen Sweet/Fotolia; 28, Ingo Wagner/EPA/Newscom; 29, MultipleParent/Wikimedia Commons; 30, de ingenium—design/Fotolia; 32, Oliver Stollman/Wikimedia Commons; 34, HultonArchive/iStock; 36, Ahavelaar/Dreamstime; 38, Carl Mikoy/Wikimedia Commons; 40, Dmitry Bokov/Fotolia; 42, Lindsay Douglas/Dreamstime; 44, Terry Schmitt/UPI/Newscom; 47, Patsy Lynch/Polaris/Newscom; 51, LightLock/iStock; 52, Pekic/iStock; 54, Frank R. Snyder/Wikimedia Commons; 61, Juanmonino/iStock
Front cover: donskarpo/iStock

UNDERSTANDING SEXUAL ORIENTATION AND GENDER IDENTITY

CONTENTS

KEY ICONS TO LOOK FOR

 Text-Dependent Questions: These questions send the reader back to the text for more careful attention to the evidence presented there.

 Words to Understand: These words with their easy-to-understand definitions will increase the reader's understanding of the text while building vocabulary skills.

 Series Glossary of Key Terms: This back-of-the-book glossary contains terminology used throughout this series. Words found here increase the reader's ability to read and comprehend higher-level books and articles in this field.

 Research Projects: Readers are pointed toward areas of further inquiry connected to each chapter. Suggestions are provided for projects that encourage deeper research and analysis.

 Sidebars: This boxed material within the main text allows readers to build knowledge, gain insights, explore possibilities, and broaden their perspectives by weaving together additional information to provide realistic and holistic perspectives.

FOREWORD

I loved libraries as a kid.

Every Saturday my mom and I would drive from the trailer where we lived on an unpaved road in the unincorporated town of Lewisville, North Carolina, and make the long drive to the "big city" of Winston-Salem to go to the downtown public library, where I would spend joyous hours perusing the books on the shelves. I'd end up lugging home as many books as my arms could carry and generally would devour them over the next seven days, all the while eagerly anticipating next week's trip. The library opened up all kinds of worlds to me—all kinds of worlds, except a gay one.

Oh, I found some "gay" books, even in the dark days of the 1970s. I'm not sure how I did, but I found my way to authors like Tennessee Williams, Yukio Mishima, and Gore Vidal. While these great artists created masterpieces of literature that affirmed that there were indeed other gay people in the universe, their portrayals of often-doomed gay men hardly made me feel hopeful about my future. It was better than nothing, but not much better. I felt so lonely and isolated I attempted to take my own life my junior year of high school.

In the 35 years since I graduated from high school in 1981, much has changed. Gay–straight alliances (an idea my students and I pioneered at Concord Academy in 1988) are now widespread in American schools. Out LGBT (lesbian, gay, bisexual, and transgender) celebrities and programs with LGBT themes are commonplace on the airwaves. Oregon has a proud bisexual governor, multiple members of Congress are out as lesbian, gay, or bisexual, and the White House was bathed in rainbow colors the day marriage equality became the law of the land in 2015. It gets better, indeed.

So why do we need the Living Proud! series?

- Because GLSEN (the Gay, Lesbian & Straight Education Network) reports that over two-thirds of LGBT students routinely hear anti-LGBT language at school.

- Because GLSEN reports that over 60% of LGBT students do not feel safe at school.
- Because the CDC (the Centers for Disease Control and Prevention, a U.S. government agency) reports that lesbian and gay students are four times more likely to attempt suicide than heterosexual students

In my current role as the executive director of the Arcus Foundation (the world's largest financial supporter of LGBT rights), I work in dozens of countries and see how far there still is to go. In over 70 countries same-sex relations are crimes under existing laws: in 8, they are a crime punishable by the death penalty. It's better, but it's not all better—especially in our libraries, where there remains a need for books that address LGBT issues that are appropriate for young people, books that will erase both the sense of isolation so many young LGBT people still feel as well as the ignorance so many non-LGBT young people have, ignorance that leads to the hate and violence that still plagues our community, both at home and abroad.

The Living Proud! series will change that and will save lives. By providing accurate, age-appropriate information to young people of all sexual orientations and gender identities, the Living Proud! series will help young people understand the complexities of the LGBT experience. Young LGBT people will see themselves in its pages, and that reflection will help them see a future full of hope and promise. I wish Living Proud! had been on the shelves of the Winston-Salem/Forsyth County Public Library back in the seventies. It would have changed my life. I'm confident that it will have as big an impact on its readers today as it would have had on me back then. And I commend it to readers of any age.

Kevin Jennings
Founder, GLSEN (the Gay, Lesbian & Straight Education Network)
Executive Director, Arcus Foundation

GLSEN®

GLSEN is the leading national education organization focused on ensuring safe and affirming schools for all students. GLSEN seeks to develop school climates where difference is valued for the positive contribution it makes to creating a more vibrant and diverse community.
www.glsen.org

The Two Friends (1894) by Henri de Toulouse-Lautrec.

UNDERSTANDING SEXUAL ORIENTATION AND GENDER IDENTITY

You can't predict a person's sexual orientation or gender identity just by looking at them.

1

THE ORIGINS OF SEXUAL ORIENTATION AND GENDER IDENTITY

 WORDS TO UNDERSTAND

Trait: A characteristic of an individual, such as eye color or gender.

Gender identity: A person's self-image as either a female or a male, no matter what gender they were assigned at birth.

Sexual orientation: A person's physical and emotional attraction to a different sex (heterosexuality), the same sex (homosexuality), both sexes (bisexuality), or neither sex (asexuality).

Hormones: Chemicals produced by the body that regulate biological functions, including male and female gender traits such as beard growth and breast development.

Are people born homosexual? Do experiences early in a person's life turn him or her gay? What causes homosexuality?

Before we can begin to answer these questions, there are some important words and concepts that must be understood. Let's start with a very basic one: What exactly do we mean by "homosexuality"?

The word *homosexuality* is made up of a Greek word, *homo*, meaning "same," and *sexuality*, which comes from the ancient Latin for *female or male*. So, very simply, *homosexuality* means *same sex*. The word was unknown before the mid-1800s, but quickly took on its modern definition: the emotional and physical attraction of a person of one sex (male or female) toward people of the same sex. *Gay* is a less scientific word, but it's the one many homosexual people prefer to use about themselves.

Like everyone else, people who are LGBT start out as babies. There they are, the next generation, behind a glass window in a hospital nursery. There are big babies, little babies, pink babies, brown babies, babies of all descriptions; some are crying, some sleeping, and some getting their first look at the world around them. Each one is a unique individual from the moment he or she is born. But the most obvious thing about those babies in the nursery—the thing you can tell right away, at least in American culture—is whether they are boy babies or girl babies. The boys are wearing little blue caps, the girls little pink ones.

In our tradition, blue is for boys and pink is for girls; these are the traditional colors of gender identification. This identification is made in the delivery room (or often even earlier, through ultrasound

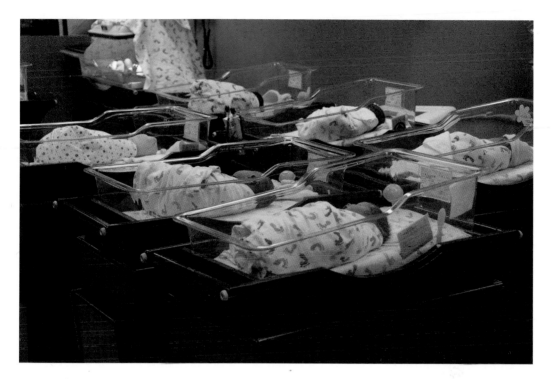

Even though these babies have just been born, already the people around them have begun making assumptions about who they are based on the gender they have been assigned.

pictures of the baby before it's born) by a quick glimpse of the baby's genitalia. "It's a boy!" or "It's a girl!" are often the first words a new mother hears. This simplest form of sex identification, the visual one, relates to the outward appearance of biological sex as determined by the baby's genitals.

Sex can be thought of as a basic biological **trait**, since male and female sexes are necessary for reproduction. Throughout the animal

Babies are often dressed based on traditional gender identities. This baby may grow up to be a person who wants nothing to do with pink frilly outfits.

kingdom, mature males produce sperm cells to fertilize the egg cells produced by mature females, and the new life produced at conception grows and matures in the female's body. But of course you know all these "facts of life" already.

Gender Roles

From the moment they are born, little girls and little boys are expected to be different from each other. What is considered to be "normal" male or female behavior varies around the world, and it has changed over the course of history, but we all know the stereotypes. Females are expected to be gentler and more emotional and sensitive. They are caregivers and nurturers. They like to dress up as princesses and play with dolls when they are little, and they grow up liking "pretty" things. Males are expected to be rougher and tougher; they don't cry easily. Boys like competitive sports and getting dirty, and they grow up wanting to be big and strong. Parents, teachers, and other authority figures almost always have different expectations for how boys and girls should act, and boys and girls are often rewarded for behaving in these gender-appropriate ways. "Boys will be boys," as the saying goes. And boys who don't act like boys are made fun of for being "sissies," while girls who like to play rough games are called "tomboys."

For some people, these gender roles are reasonably comfortable. For many others, however, these roles can be uncomfortable to take on. Luckily, gender roles have changed in recent years, becoming less rigid, as women have gained greater gender equality. Indeed, both men and women today have more freedom to behave outside the stricter gender roles of the past. Slowly, our culture is realizing that the way human beings experience their gender is a lot more complex than we originally thought. Suffice it to say: we don't all fit comfortably into the roles associated with our assigned gender—no matter how "natural" they may seem to others.

Transgender

A person's biological sex is not necessarily the same thing as his or her **gender identity**. According to the Human Rights Campaign, the largest LGBT political organization in the world, up to 1 percent of the adult population does not feel comfortable with the gender roles and physical traits of the sex they were assigned at birth. These people are referred to as *transgender,* and growing up transgender can be a very challenging experience.

"I just never felt comfortable in my own body," explains Marty, a transgender male who was considered female when he was born. "I was forced to wear dresses and do all kinds of 'girl' things—but as far back as I remember, I knew I was a boy. I just knew it."

Marty always identified with other males and wanted to do "boy" stuff, such as play competitive sports and build things with tools.

"I started living as a man full time when I got out of the military, and I started on male **hormones** when I was twenty-five. I can't tell you how thrilled I was when my beard started to grow in. And my therapist and my transgender support group were with me every step of the way."

Besides taking hormones, some transgender people undergo gender affirmation surgery, which can be a long and very expensive series of operations. They may also go through the process of legally changing their names and gender in official records.

Marty has had his first two surgeries in his transition to becoming the biological male he feels he always was, and he is saving his money for

In India, Bangladesh, and Pakistan, hijras are usually assigned male at birth but choose a female gender identity. They are generally accepted by the larger society, though discrimination and prejudice still exist.

his next operation. (Some health insurance companies have taken steps toward covering gender affirmation procedures, but there is still a lot of progress to be made.)

"I've had to give up a lot," says Marty. "Some of my family members still won't accept that I'm not 'Martha,' and I've lost friends because I'm transgender. But I am who I am. I'm not trapped in the wrong body anymore."

Homosexuality

People who experience sexual attraction toward people of their own gender, rather than to the opposite sex, are considered homosexual.

The reason why the majority of people in the world are heterosexual (sexually attracted to people of a different gender) is fairly obvious.

 CLOSE-UP: INTERSEX

As many as one in every thousand babies is born with either external genitalia or internal sexual organs that are not clearly either female or male. These people are known as *intersex*. In the past, doctors often made a decision—sometimes even without the parents' permission—to perform surgery to "normalize" an intersex child, even though it might not have been clear which gender the child might grow up to be. Sometimes people who have been "assigned" a male or female gender early in life, either by surgery or by a decision by their doctors and parents, grow up with serious gender confusion and identity problems. The Intersex Society of North America is an organization that advocates for informed choice, educating doctors and parents about intersex issues and assisting intersex people with the challenges they face. Many intersex people live happy and satisfying lives outside of the "normal" female and male gender identities.

Lili Elbe was one of the first people to have gender affirmation surgery. Assigned male at her birth in Denmark in 1882, she travelled to Germany in 1930 for a series of experimental surgeries. She died in 1931 from complications related to her fifth surgery, a uterus transplant that she hoped would allow her to have children.

A child can grow up happy and well adjusted with a single parent, two parents of the same sex, or two parents of different sex.

2

BORN GAY: BIOLOGICAL THEORIES OF HOMOSEXUALITY

 WORDS TO UNDERSTAND

Gene: A microscopic sequence of DNA located within a chromosome that determines a particular biological characteristic, such as eye color.
Inborn: Traits, whether visible or not, that are a part of who we are at birth.
Conclusive: The final answer to a question or problem, based on proof that can't be questioned.
Theories: Ideas or explanations based on research, experimentation, and evidence.
Prenatal: Before birth; the nine-month period during which a baby develops within its mother's body.

Are gay people born gay? Is there a homosexual **gene**? Is there a basic biological reason why some people are attracted to members of their own sex? Are gay people biologically "different" from straight people? Research on these questions has been going on for many years, mostly by scientists on the "nature" side of the nature-versus-nurture debate.

Genetics is the study of the inheritance of biological traits, the passing on of physical and other **inborn** characteristics from parents to their children through the process of sexual reproduction. So how does it work?

A Quick Lesson in Genetics

The basic building blocks of genetics are genes, carried on microscopic strands of genetic material called chromosomes. The twenty-three chromosomes contained in the male's sperm and twenty-three found in the female's egg come together in unique combinations when the sperm fertilizes the egg in a process called *conception*. A child's biological parents each contribute exactly half of the genes that carry all the new baby's potential biological characteristics. The way these genes combine—which is unique in every conception (except in identical twins, as we shall see)—determines which particular biological traits the baby will inherit from its parents.

Full biological brothers and sisters have access to the same genetic material from their parents, but these genes can combine together in a nearly infinite number of ways. This means that brothers and sisters tend to have some similar traits while others are very different. However, because identical twins develop from a single fertilized egg (and the same combination of the same forty-six chromosomes), they are genetically

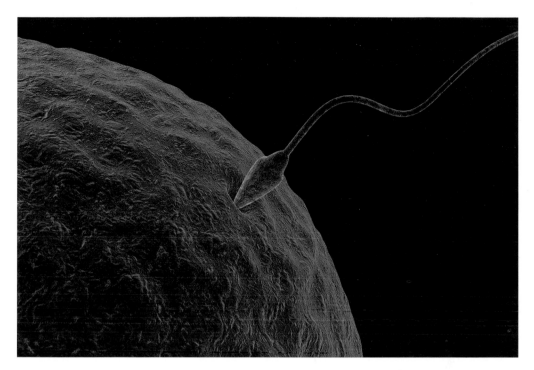

From the instant the sperm fertilizes the egg, many of our biological characteristics have already been determined.

identical. If there is a gay gene, or more likely a combination of genes that causes homosexuality, identical twins should be likely to share the same sexual orientation. That's why studies of twins have been of great interest to scientists studying this question.

Genetics and Homosexuality

A major study by psychologist Michael Bailey from Northwestern University and psychiatrist Richard Pillard from the Boston University School of Medicine found that if one male identical twin was gay, there

CLOSE-UP: HOMOSEXUALITY IN THE ANIMAL KINGDOM

Homosexuality isn't just for humans: It can be found throughout the animal kingdom. Homosexual behavior has been observed in close to 1,500 species and is well-documented in over 500, including black swans, mallard ducks, and penguins, as well as apes, elephants, giraffes, sheep, hyenas, lizards, and even fruit flies!

Male-on-male sexual behavior is sometimes used as a show of dominance, but it is usually simply friendly and playful. Eight percent of sheep show a homosexual preference, and same-sex penguin pairs mate for life and sometimes even raise orphaned chicks together. Researcher Petter Bøckman has written, "No species has been found in which homosexual behavior has not been shown to exist, with the exception of species that never have sex at all, such as sea urchins." While some anti-gay people say that homosexuality is a "crime against nature," nature seems to feel differently!

Some male penguins have been discovered to prefer the company of other males, and in fact, have remained together as mates for life.

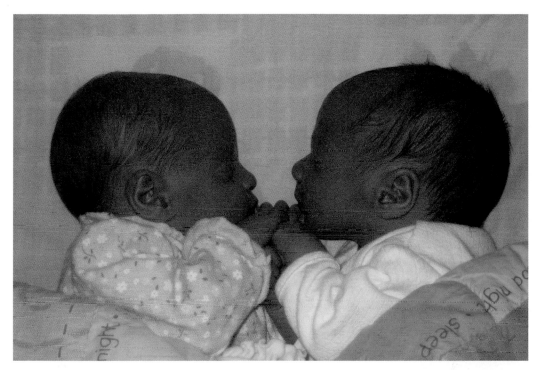

While twins can share many of the same traits, they may also be different in important ways. Traits are caused by a variety of factors, including genetics and environment.

was a 52 percent chance that the other twin would be, too. In the case of fraternal (non-identical) twins, if one twin was gay there was a 27 percent chance that the other twin was also gay. A large-scale study of lesbian twins yielded similar results (48 percent for identical twins, 16 percent for fraternal twins). Other twin studies have supported these findings. In other words, there does appear to be a genetic component to sexual orientation.

Scientists have also looked at how many gay people there are in an extended family. The results of some of these studies indicate that homosexuality seems to be more common in some families than in others and that there is a possibility that people inherit their "gay genes" from their mother's side of the family, since it turns out that a gay person's maternal cousins are more likely to be gay than would be expected in a random sample of family members.

While these twin and family studies are far from **conclusive,** they do strongly suggest that there is at least some, and probably a significant, genetic influence on homosexuality. Meanwhile, geneticists continue to investigate the subject, and some think they are near to achieving proof.

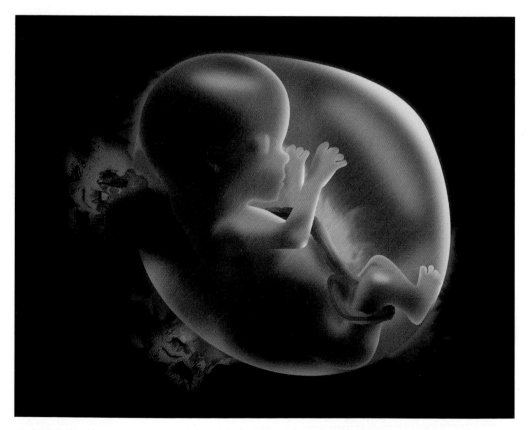

Before a baby is born, its mother's hormone levels may affect its development.

Prenatal Influences

But even if being homosexual is not a genetic trait—and no specific "gay gene" has yet been found—there are other biological **theories** about what makes people gay, theories that look at what goes on inside a mother's body during the nine months her baby is developing. **Prenatal** sex hormone levels may differ at significant times during a woman's pregnancy, her health and her environment may affect the development of the baby, and certain genes are known to "turn on" or "turn off" for unknown reasons. The reason scientists have looked for a prenatal cause for homosexuality is the fact that some studies have shown that certain other biological traits—unrelated to sexual orientation—are more common in gay people than in the straight population. Here are a few results from these trait studies:

- Left-handedness is one-third more common (31 percent) in gay men and twice as common among lesbians (91 percent) than among straight people.
- The left half of the brain is larger than the right in the majority of gay men and heterosexual women, while the right half is larger in lesbians and heterosexual men.
- Gay men tend to score higher than straight men in tests of language ability, while lesbians score similarly to heterosexual men and higher than straight women in spatial ability (the understanding of objects in physical space).
- The index and ring fingers of gay men and heterosexual women tend to be the same length, while in straight men and lesbians the index finger is usually longer.

These studies are also far from conclusive, but some of these findings (brain size and finger length, for example) may be related to the levels of male hormones to which the developing baby is exposed. Developing female babies exposed to high levels of male hormones at a certain time during their mother's pregnancy may be more likely to become lesbians, and male babies exposed to lower levels may be more likely to be gay when they grow up.

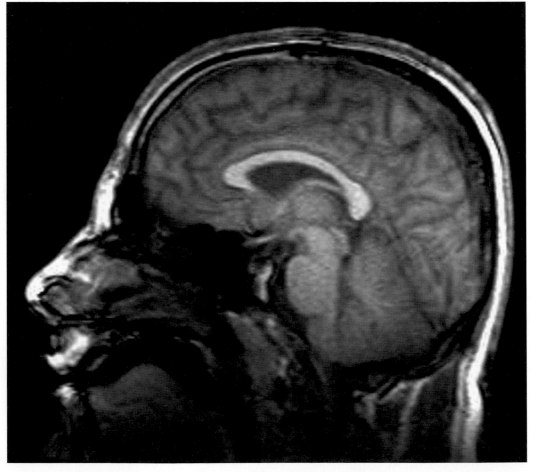

Some scientists think the structure of the brain has a lot to do with a person's sexual orientation.

Born That Way

But it's not as simple as gay men being more like heterosexual women and lesbians more like heterosexual men. Early experiments in which gay men were given large doses of male hormones in order to make them more "manly" were a failure. High levels of male hormones simply increased the sex drive of these men without changing who they were attracted to.

What can we conclude from all of these twin studies, family studies, and research on physical traits common to gay people? They all seem to indicate quite strongly—if not prove—that there is a biological cause for homosexuality. Dr. Qazi Rahman, a lecturer in biology at the University of London who was involved in the brain-size study we mentioned, says of his research, "As far as I'm concerned, there is no argument any more—if you are gay, you are born gay."

 TEXT-DEPENDENT QUESTIONS

- If one identical twin is gay, how likely is it that the other will be, too?
- If one fraternal twin is gay, how likely is it that the other will be, too?
- How has an influx of male hormones been shown to affect gay male behavior?

RESEARCH PROJECTS

- Use the Internet to search out various theories of what causes homosexuality.
- Read about recent studies that appear to confirm a genetic link to homosexuality.

How a child is raised does not determine his or her gender identity or sexual orientation.

3

BECOMING GAY: PSYCHOLOGICAL THEORIES OF HOMOSEXUALITY

 WORDS TO UNDERSTAND

Psychologists and psychiatrists: Professionals who study and treat the human mind and human behavior. Psychiatrists are medical doctors, whereas psychologists are not.

Disorder: A mental or physical disease.

Intervention: An organized effort to help someone by changing their attitudes or behavior.

Stereotypes: Ways of thinking about people not based on who they are but on the expected behavior of the group they belong to.

The "nurture" side of the debate about what causes homosexuality brings us to the very complex science of the human mind and human behavior called psychology. For many years, **psychologists** and **psychiatrists**

LGBT couples can marry and have children if they choose.

have studied how sexual orientation may be more a matter of mind than of biology.

Homosexuality as a "Mental Disorder"

The scientific study of the human mind is only a little over a hundred years old. One of its famous founders, the Austrian psychiatrist Sigmund Freud (1856–1939), believed that all human beings were basically bisexual and that a person's adult sexual orientation, whether heterosexual or homosexual, was largely the result of his or her early-childhood experiences. However, although Freud believed that homosexuality was a normal human sexual behavior, it took many years before the field of study he helped establish caught up with his progressive ideas.

For much of the twentieth century, most psychologists and psychiatrists classified homosexuality as a serious mental illness and considered homosexuals to be sick and abnormal. Medical science supported the church and the legal system in the oppression of gay and lesbian people. Homosexuals were not only considered sinners and criminals, they were thought to be sick, too. They were committed to mental hospitals by the thousands and subjected to "treatments" that included being shot up with drugs and hormones, given electroshock therapy, and even subjected to brain surgery. Is it any wonder that LGBT people were often described by doctors as lonely, unhappy, and suicidal?

Thousands of gay men and women underwent years of long, psychologically painful therapy with doctors who told them they were deeply sick and could never live happy, fulfilling lives unless they were "cured." In *Cures: A Gay Man's Odyssey*, the historian and gay activist Martin Duberman tells

As recently as the middle of the 20th century, homosexuals could be committed against their will to psychiatric hospitals, such as Bellevue in New York City, shown here. Not until 1973 did the American Psychiatric Association remove homosexuality from its list of mental disorders.

a sadly typical story of deep frustration with the psychiatric profession in the 1950s, as he sought help in dealing with his own homosexuality.

The bad old days of treating homosexuals as sick started to improve in the 1960s and, at a historic meeting in 1973, the American Psychiatric Association (APA) removed homosexuality as a mental **disorder** from its *Diagnostic and Statistical Manual of Mental Disorders* (DSM-II) in response to pressure from the newly organized gay liberation movement.

Most LGBT people have made their peace with the mental health profession that was once part of a system that oppressed and misunderstood them. In fact, many thousands of LGBT people work in the mental health field today, and many more have had positive, supportive experiences in therapy.

But even if homosexuality is no longer considered a "mental disorder" by most of the scientific community, the reason *why* a certain percentage of people are gay continues to interest researchers in human behavior.

 CLOSE-UP: APA REJECTS CONVERSION THERAPY

At their 2009 meeting, the American Psychological Association declared that mental health professionals should not tell gay clients that they can become straight through therapy or other treatments. In a resolution adopted by the association's governing council in a 125-to-4 vote, the association issued a rejection of what is called "reparative" or "conversion" therapy, a treatment practiced by a small but vocal group of therapists (often religious conservatives) who maintain that gay men and lesbians can change. No solid evidence exists that such change is possible, says the resolution.

The association went on to say that some research suggests that efforts to produce change can be harmful, causing depression and suicidal thoughts. Instead of seeking such change, the association urged therapists to consider multiple options, including celibacy and switching churches, for helping clients to live spiritually rewarding lives in instances where their sexual orientation and religious faith are in conflict. The association had criticized reparative therapy in the past, but a six-member panel added weight to that position by examining eighty-three studies on sexual orientation change conducted since 1960.

Interacting Causes

In the last twenty years, LGBT people themselves, along with a majority of scientists, have been rejecting these theories as simplistic. As gay and lesbian people have come out in large numbers, they have come to understand—and have been teaching their straight friends and families—that the tired old **stereotypes** of sissy men who were "too close" to their mothers and women "who want to be men"

The toys a child enjoys playing with have nothing to do with his or her sexual orientation.

do not represent the diversity of the gay community or the real-life experiences of most gays and lesbians. Many gay men are not "sissy boys," and many enjoy strong, positive relationships with their fathers; lots of gay women had no gender-role conflicts as little girls. (And, on the flip side, lots of **effeminate** men are happily heterosexual, and many "tomboy" little girls grow up to be enthusiastically attracted to the opposite sex.)

Out-and-proud LGBT people in the twenty-first century feel comfortable rejecting the roles of "girly men" and "manly women" that are still powerful stereotypes of gay people. And, maybe even more important, they feel free to exhibit these characteristics if they come naturally. What's *wrong* with being a "sissy boy" or "tomboy," and why would parents want to train a child *not* to be one, if that is what he or she was meant to be?

There is no clear psychological explanation of why some people are homosexual. Early-life experiences and family relationships may have an effect on sexual orientation, but human behavior is such a complex combination of mind and brain—the psychological and the biological working together—that it is nearly impossible to separate the two. So the real question is: why does it matter what causes homosexuality?

You can lead a happy and productive life being who you are.

TEXT-DEPENDENT QUESTIONS

- What did Sigmund Freud cite as the cause of homosexuality?

- When did the American Psychiatric Association remove homosexuality from its list of mental disorders?

- Are masculine women and effeminate men always homosexual?

RESEARCH PROJECTS

- Talk to some out gay people about their upbringing, their relationships with their parents, and whether they think "nurture" (their family and environment) had any role in shaping their sexuality.

- Check out the American Psychological Association's web page on sexual orientation and homosexuality.

Marriage equality, which became law in the United States in 2015 after a landmark Supreme Court decision, was an important blow to prejudice and discrimination against LGBT people.

4

WHY DOES IT MATTER?

 WORDS TO UNDERSTAND

Allies: People on the same side, who support the same things.
Perception: The way a person looks at and understands a situation.
Status: The position of something in comparison to something else.
Legitimized: Being taken seriously and having the support of large numbers of people.
Opponents: People who oppose or are against something.
Conservatives: People who tend to be against change and new ideas in society.

Nature or nurture? Genetics, biology, or psychology? By now, you must have gotten the message that there are no absolutely clear answers as to what causes homosexuality. And, while some people outside the gay community want to argue that being gay is a choice, we can quickly eliminate that particular "cause" simply by asking gay people why they think they are gay. Many, perhaps most, gay people knew that they were "different" at a very young age, many long before they had even heard the word "gay." Most gay people believe they were born gay, because their "gayness" has always felt like such a basic and natural part of who they are. Very few gay people, however, can even imagine what it would mean to "choose" to be homosexual. Ask yourself: Do you think people choose to be heterosexual?

One thing does seem clear: A person's sexual orientation is as basic to who he is as the color of his eyes (and you know you didn't chose that).

So why does it matter what causes homosexuality, any more than it matters what causes heterosexuality?

Through the political efforts of LGBT people themselves, and with the help of their **allies**, the LGBT community has come a long way in recent years toward acceptance in society with full legal and civil rights. But the struggle continues, and LGBT people will always remain a minority group within the majority population. While one of the most important responsibilities of government in a free society is to protect the rights of minority groups from oppression by the majority, gay people still do not have all of the same rights that straight people do. For example, they are not fully protected from being fired from their jobs because of their sexual orientation; in certain states, they cannot adopt children; and only recently have they been granted the right to serve openly in the military. These are all rights that straight people take for granted. Unlike any other minority group in

The gay community has made significant progress in the fight to serve openly in the military. Shown here is a program from the 2015 Department of Defense Lesbian, Gay, Bisexual, and Transgender Pride Month ceremony at the Pentagon. The Secretary of Defense delivered the keynote address in which he announced that gay and lesbian troops for the first time would be protected from discrimination by the Pentagon's equal opportunity policy. The change ensures that gay and lesbian troops' complaints about discrimination based on sexual orientation will be investigated by the Military Equal Opportunity program, the same office that handles complaints based on race, color, religion sex or national origin. Unfortunately, at the time of this writing, there is still a ban on transgender people serving in the military. Many expect this ban to be lifted sometime soon, but its existence is a clear indication of the significant oppression faced by transgender people in the United States today.

America, LGBT people are in a strange position where certain rights legally granted to them by the courts can be taken away from them by the vote of the majority.

Homosexuality and Legal Rights

Can you imagine if the voting rights of Black Americans, a right granted to them by the Supreme Court of the United States, could be taken away if a majority of White people voted on it? Or, what if all the blondes and brunettes in the world could vote that red-haired people not be allowed to get married and have children? Can you imagine what it would be like to have *your* rights taken away by a majority vote?

One of the reasons that LGBT people have had to fight so hard for "equal protection under the law" may be the **perception** of the majority—from the scientific community to the average person—of the LGBT community's **status** as a minority group. It seems that the best way for a minority group to be perceived as *deserving* the full rights and privileges enjoyed by the majority is if people are a part of that minority by birth—in other words, through no fault of their own! After all, we don't choose our skin color or our ethnic background.

Children born to African American parents can be physically identified as Black Americans by the color of their skin, but LGBT people are an invisible minority. That is, LGBT people cannot be recognized by the way they look or speak or act (even if some people claim to have "gaydar" or make snap judgments based on those tired stereotypes we talked about). Gay people are usually born to "majority" heterosexual parents, and they can choose to identify themselves openly as gay or keep the fact private, as they wish. But if it could be proven that being gay is an inborn genetic or biological trait, the minority status of gay people would be strongly **legitimized**.

It is much harder for the straight majority to argue that a law-abiding, tax-paying minority made up of people *born* gay does not deserve their full rights as citizens, including fair and equal treatment under the law. Gay rights become, then, a simple matter of fairness!

But even if a biological basis for homosexuality remains in question, in a society that values fairness, it's not legitimate to deny people their rights based on behaviors that do not harm other people and that are private and deeply personal. So, while maybe not quite as strong as the biological argument, a psychological cause for homosexuality still strongly supports gay people's status as a minority group deserving the full legal rights that other minority groups (not to mention the majority) enjoy.

Religion and Homosexuality

The strongest **opponents** of LGBT rights, religious and political **conservatives**, still argue that being gay is a choice—despite the fact that most of the scientific community and most gay people themselves strongly disagree with them. For many religious conservatives, same-sex relationships are a serious offense, a sin against God, and people who engage in these are considered sinners. Organized religious groups continue to fight against the rights of LGBT people at the local, state, and national levels. Meanwhile, through the "ex-gay ministries" they support, they continue to subject unhappy, conflicted gay people to psychologically harmful therapies in an attempt to change their sexual orientation.

 CLOSE-UP: CHRISTIAN ACCEPTANCE OF GAY NATURE

Religious opponents to LGBT rights cite the Old Testament's Book of Leviticus, passage 20:13, which calls sexual relations between men an "abomination." There are several rebuttals to this, the most obvious of which is that U.S. law is not based on scripture. Perhaps more powerful are the overtly Christian responses, which stress kindness, inclusion, and increasing recognition of sexual nature as innate.

Desmond Tutu, the Anglican Archbishop Emeritus of South Africa and a social rights activist, put it most eloquently when he said, "We reject [homosexuals], treat them as pariahs, and push them outside our church communities, and thereby we negate the consequences of their baptism and ours. We make them doubt that they are the children of God, and this must be nearly the ultimate blasphemy. We blame them for something that is becoming increasingly clear they can do little about."

Love

In the end, though, does it really matter what causes homosexuality? Being gay is really all about who a person loves. Even if you don't happen to agree with a person's choice in this most personal and private

Desmond Tutu, the Anglican Archbishop Emeritus of South Africa and a civil rights activist, has eloquently called for church and community to embrace LGBT people as "children of God" like everyone else.

The reality of a couple's relationship should not be affected by the opinions of others. Love is love, wherever you find it.

matter, do you have the right to deny another person's happiness? Does America have the right to deny a portion of its citizens their full legal and civil rights because the so-called majority doesn't "approve" of their lifestyle?

These are the real questions to be asking in the 21st century. And, as LGBT people continue to live open, proud, and productive lives and their straight friends and families continue to love and respect them for who they are, the future of personal freedom and "the pursuit of happiness" looks brighter for all of us. As the saying goes, "Love conquers all."

 TEXT-DEPENDENT QUESTIONS

- What is the major difference between LGBT people and other minority groups?
- What are the likely reasons that LGBT people have had to fight so hard for their rights?
- What is the principal argument of those who oppose LGBT rights?

 RESEARCH PROJECTS

- Ask some out LGBT people whether they think being LGBT is a choice. If they say no, ask if they *would* choose to be LGBT, if it were.
- Check out the laws in your state or community with regard to LGBT people; see if there are any restrictions on housing, employment, or adoption.

⬚ SERIES GLOSSARY

Activists: People committed to social change through political and personal action.

Advocacy: The process of supporting the rights of a group of people and speaking out on their behalf.

Alienation: A feeling of separation and distance from other people and from society.

Allies: People who support others in a cause.

Ambiguous: Something unclear or confusing.

Anonymous: Being unknown; having no one know who you are.

Assumption: A conclusion drawn without the benefit of real evidence.

Backlash: An adverse reaction by a large number of people, especially to a social or political development.

Bias: A tendency or preference toward a particular perspective or ideology that interferes with the ability to be impartial, unprejudiced, or objective.

Bigotry: Stubborn and complete intolerance of a religion, appearance, belief, or ethnic background that differs from one's own.

Binary: A system made up of two, and only two, parts.

Bohemian: Used to describe movements, people, or places characterized by nontraditional values and ways of life often coupled with an interest in the arts and political movements.

Caricature: An exaggerated representation of a person.

Celibate: Choosing not to have sex.

Chromosome: A microscopic thread of genes within a cell that carries all the information determining what a person is like, including his or her sex.

Cisgender: Someone who self-identifies with the gender he or she was assigned at birth.

Civil rights: The rights of a citizen to personal and political freedom under the law.

Clichés: Expressions that have become so overused—stereotypes, for example—that they tend to be used without thought.

Closeted: Choosing to conceal one's true sexual orientation or gender identity.

Compensating: Making up for something by trying harder or going further in the opposite direction.

Conservative: Cautious; resistant to change and new ideas.

Controversy: A disagreement, often involving a touchy subject about which differing opinions create tension and strong reactions.

Customs: Ideas and ways of doing things that are commonly understood and shared within a society.

Demonize: Portray something or someone as evil.

Denominations: Large groups of religious congregations united under a common faith and name, and organized under a single legal administration.

Derogatory: Critical or cruel, as in a term used to make a person feel devalued or humiliated.

Deviation: Something abnormal; something that has moved away from the standard.

Dichotomy: Division into two opposite and contradictory groups.

Discrimination: When someone is treated differently because of his or her race, sexual orientation, gender identity, religion, or some other factor.

Disproportionate: A situation where one particular group is overrepresented within a larger group.

Diverse: In the case of a community, one that is made up of people from many different backgrounds.

Effeminate: A word used to refer to men who have so-called feminine qualities.

Emasculated: Having had one's masculinity or manhood taken away.

Empathy: Feeling for another person; putting yourself mentally and emotionally in another person's place.

Empirical evidence: Factual data gathered from direct observation.

Empowering: Providing strength and energy; making someone feel powerful.

Endocrinologist: A medical doctor who specializes in the treatment of hormonal issues.

Epithets: Words or terms used in a derogatory way to put a person down.

The Establishment: The people who hold influence and power in society.

Extremist: Someone who is in favor of using extreme or radical measures, especially in politics and religion.

Flamboyant: Colorful and a bit outrageous.

Fundamentalist: Someone who believes in a particular religion's fundamental principles and follows them rigidly. When the word is used in connection with Christianity, it refers to a member of a form of Protestant Christianity that believes in the strict and literal interpretation of the Bible.

Gay liberation: The movement for the civil and legal rights of gay people that originated in the 1950s and emerged as a potent force for social and political change in the late 1960s and '70s.

Gender: A constructed sexual identity, whether masculine, feminine, or entirely different.

Gender identity: A person's self-image as female, male, or something entirely different, no matter what gender a person was assigned at birth.

Gender roles: Those activities and traits that are considered appropriate to males and females within a given culture.

Gene: A microscopic sequence of DNA located within a chromosome that determines a particular biological characteristic, such as eye color.

Genitalia: The scientific term for the male and female sex organs.

Genocide: The large-scale murder and destruction of a particular group of people.

Grassroots: At a local level; usually used in reference to political action that begins within a community rather than on a national or global scale.

Harassed/harassment: Being teased, bullied, or physically threatened.

Hate crime: An illegal act in which the victim is targeted because of his or her race, religion, sexual orientation, or gender identity.

Homoerotic: Having to do with homosexual, or same-sex, love and desire.

Homophobia: The fear and hatred of homosexuality. A homophobic person is sometimes referred to as a "homophobe."

Horizontal hostility: Negative feeling among people within the same minority group.

Hormones: Chemicals produced by the body that regulate biological functions, including male and female gender traits, such as beard growth and breast development.

Identity: The way a person, or a group of people, defines and understands who they are.

Inborn: Traits, whether visible or not, that are a part of who we are at birth.

Inclusive: Open to all ideas and points of view.

Inhibitions: Feelings of guilt and shame that keep us from doing things we might otherwise want to do.

Internalized: Taken in; for example, when a person believes the negative opinions other people have of him, he has *internalized* their point of view and made it his own.

Interpretation: A particular way of understanding something.

Intervention: An organized effort to help people by changing their attitudes or behavior.

Karma: The force, recognized by both Hindus and Buddhists, that emanates from one's actions in this life; the concept that the good and bad things one does determine where he or she will end up in the next life.

Legitimized: Being taken seriously and having the support of large numbers of people.

LGBT: An initialism that stands for lesbian, gay, bisexual, and transgender. Sometimes a "Q" is added (**LGBTQ**) to include "questioning." "Q" may also stand for "queer."

Liberal: Open to new ideas; progressive; accepting and supportive of the ideas or identity of others.

Liberation: The act of being set free from oppression and persecution.

Mainstream: Accepted, understood, and supported by the majority of people.

Malpractice: When a doctor or other professional gives bad advice or treatment, either out of ignorance or deliberately.

Marginalize: Push someone to the sidelines, away from the rest of the world.

Mentor: Someone who teaches and offers support to another, often younger, person.

Monogamous: Having only one sexual or romantic partner.

Oppress: Keep another person or group of people in an inferior position.

Ostracized: Excluded from the rest of a group.

Out: For an LGBT person, the state of being open with other people about his or her sexual orientation or gender identity.

Outed: Revealed or exposed as LGBT against one's will.

Persona: A character or personality chosen by a person to change the way others perceive them.

Pioneers: People who are the first to try new things and experiment with new ways of life.

Politicized: Aware of one's rights and willing to demand them through political action.

Prejudice: An opinion (usually unfavorable) of a person or a group of people not based on actual knowledge.

Proactive: Taking action taken in advance of an anticipated situation or difficulty.

Progressive: Supporting human freedom and progress.

Psychologists and psychiatrists: Professionals who study the human mind and human behavior. Psychiatrists are medical doctors who can prescribe pills, whereas clinical psychologists provide talk therapy.

Quackery: When an untrained person gives medical advice or treatment, pretending to be a doctor or other medical expert.

The Right: In politics and religion, the side that is generally against social change and new ideas; often used interchangeably with *conservative*.

Segregation: Historically, a system of laws and customs that limited African Americans' access to many businesses, public spaces, schools, and neighborhoods that were "white only."

Sexual orientation: A person's physical and emotional attraction to the opposite sex (heterosexuality), the same sex (homosexuality), both sexes (bisexuality), or neither (asexuality).

Sociologists: People who study the way groups of humans behave.

Spectrum: A wide range of variations.

Stereotype: A caricature; a way to judge someone, probably unfairly, based on opinions you may have about a particular group they belong to.

Stigma: A mark of shame.

Subculture: A smaller group of people with similar interests and lifestyles within a larger group.

Taboo: Something that is forbidden.

Theories: Ideas or explanations based on research, experimentation, and evidence.

Tolerance: Acceptance of, and respect for, other people's differences.

Transgender: People who identify with a gender different from the one they were assigned at birth.

Transphobia: Fear or hatred of transgender people.

Variance: A range of differences within a category such as gender.

Victimized: Subjected to unfair and negative treatment, including violence, bullying, harassment, or prejudice.

FURTHER RESOURCES

What Is Gender Identity?
A primer on gender identity for teens.
gayteens.about.com/od/glbtbasicsforteens/f/whatisgenderid.htm

Gender Roles in Society
A global perspective on the issue.
http://www.buzzle.com/articles/gender-roles-in-society.html

Gay Twin Studies
A closer examination of the phenomenon.
gaylife.about.com/b/2007/08/03/gay-twins.htm

Facts About Homosexuality and Mental Health
A comprehensive overview of the subject.
psychology.ucdavis.edu/rainbow/html/facts_mental_health.html

Sexual Orientation and Homosexuality
The American Psychological Association's dedicated page on the issue.
http://www.apa.org/helpcenter/sexual-orientation.aspx

APA Removes Homosexuality from List of Mental Disorders
A brief history of the momentous decision.
http://www.boxturtlebulletin.com/2008/12/15/7128

Civil Rights and LGBT People
The American Civil Liberties Union's assessment of the various battlegrounds.
http://www.aclu.org/lgbt-rights

INDEX